Samsung
Galaxy Fold
User's Guide

A practical guide with advanced tips and tricks
to master your Samsung Galaxy Fold

SCOTT DOWNING

Goodwater Publishing
279 Stoney Lane
Dallas, TX 75212
Texas
USA

CONTENTS

INTRODUCTION

Galaxy Fold is Samsung's first foldable smartphone. As the name implies, the smartphone can fold and open to become smaller and bigger respectively. Literally, it puts together the portability of smartphones and utility of tablets in one piece. In its foldable state, it's a smartphone, upon unfolding, it becomes an attractive tablet.

FEATURES

Design

The foldable Samsung Galaxy Fold is designed with a sophisticated hinge system with multiple interlocking gears, hidden inside the spine. This multiple interlocking gear hinge mechanism makes the device open smoothly like a book, and close similarly with a convenient magnetic click. The fold was tested using a series of machines that repeatedly fold and unfold the phone to about 200,000 times. Galaxy Fold comes in four colors: Cosmos Black, Space Silver, Martian Green and Astro Blue. The size and weight of the Galaxy Fold are 160.90mm x 62.80mm x 17.10mm and 276 grams respectively.

There are two speakers, one at the top and one at the bottom, and it's easy to cover up these powerful Dolby Atmos stereo speakers when you're playing games or watching videos in landscape orientation.

Displays

Galaxy Fold has two foldable displays which go from a 4.6 inch display for a phone mode (folded state) to a 7.3 inch display for a tablet mode (unfolded state). The 4.6 inch display has a Super AMOLED panel with a resolution of 1680 x 720 pixels, while the 7.3 inch display has a Dynamic AMOLED panel with a resolution of 2152 x 1536 pixels.

Camera

There are six cameras on the Galaxy Fold. There's a 10-megapixel lens on the front, as well as a 10-megapixel lens paired with an 8-megapixel 3D depth sensor on the front when the screen is unfolded. On the rear, you'll find a 16-megapixel ultrawide lens, a 12-megapixel standard lens (with variable aperture), and a 12-megapixel telephoto lens.

Hardware and Software

Galaxy Fold smartphone runs on Android v9.0 (Pie) operating system. The device is powered by 8 core (2.84 GHz, Single core, Kryo 485 + 2.42 GHz, Tri core, Kryo 485 + 1.7 GHz, Quad core, Kryo 485) processor. It runs on the Qualcomm Snapdragon 855 Chipset and Adreno 640 GPU. It has 12 GB RAM and 512 GB internal storage. The Galaxy Fold features such built-in sensors as Accelerometer, Barometer, Optical Fingerprint Sensor, Gyro Sensor,

Geomagnatic Sensor, Hall Sensor, Heart Rate Sensor, Proximity Sensor and RGB Light Sensor. Some smart softwares made their way into the device. They include but not limited to the following:

- **App continuity**

App Continuity enables you to open an app on the cover display and then have the same app immediately fill the larger screen when you unfold the phone. For instance, if you're using an app like Google Maps on the front screen, you can open the display and it will instantly fill the larger display.

- **3-App multitasking**

3-App multitasking or Multi window allows you to run up to three apps simultaneously in a split-screen on the Galaxy Fold's large display.

- **Bixby**

Bixby is a virtual assistant that learns, evolves and adapts to you. It learns your routines, helps you set up reminders based on time and location, and is built in to your favorite apps.

Battery

The Galaxy Fold comes with a 4,380 mAh dual battery, which has a customized built-in technology to combine the energy from the two batteries into one power source. Each of the two batteries is found on either side of the sophisticated hinge, and they are non-removable. The batteries are charged using the USB-C cable with an input of

18W power. Also, you can charge other devices wirelessly with the phone thanks to Wireless Powershare.

GETTING STARTED

UNBOXING YOUR GALAXY FOLD

What are the accessories that come with the Galaxy Fold? Make sure to look inside its box and take everything out. This is what is expected to be inside every Galaxy Fold box:

1. **Galaxy Buds**: A pair of Galaxy Buds that can wirelessly connect to your phone.

2. **Aramid Fiber Cover**: A feather light, indomitable case that's perfectly tailored to protect the Galaxy Fold.

3. **Travel adapter**: The charger adapter that you plug into the wall.

4. **USB cable**: Use the Type-C USB cable that connects the adapter to your phone.

5. **USB connector**: Used for changing the Type-C USB port to a Type-B USB.

6. **Ejector tool**: Used for ejecting the SIM tray.

DEVICE LAYOUT

Outside Layout

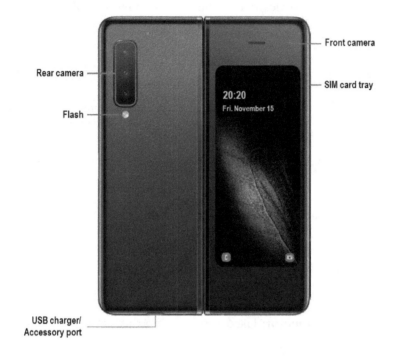

Rear camera

Flash

Front camera

SIM card tray

20:20
Fri. November 15

USB charger/
Accessory port

Inside Layout

Speaker

Volume Keys

Power Key

Bixby Key/
Fingerprint
scanner

Speaker

CHARGING THE BATTERY

It's very important that you charge the battery before using it for the first time or when it has been unused for extended periods. Always use only Samsung-approved battery, charger, and cable specifically designed for your device. This will help to maximize your battery life. Incompatible battery, charger, and cable can cause serious injuries or damage to your device. Use only USB Type-C cable supplied with the device. Follow the steps below to charge your Galaxy Fold.

1. Connect the USB cable to the USB power adaptor.
2. Plug the USB cable into the device's multipurpose jack.

3. Plug the USB power adaptor into an electric socket.

4. After fully charging, disconnect the charger from the device. Then, unplug the charger from the electric socket.

Wireless PowerShare

Wirelessly charge your compatible Samsung devices using your phone. Some features are not available while sharing power.

Wireless PowerShare is a feature available on Galaxy Fold that turns the device into a Qi wireless charger and charges other devices that support the standard, like the Galaxy Buds earbuds case, or even a smart Watch. It's best used in dire situations, as it's slow. To use the Wireless PowerShare feature, follow these steps to charge other compatible devices.

1. From Quick Settings, tap **Wireless PowerShare**.

2. With the phone face down, place the compatible device on the back of the phone to charge. A notification sound or vibration occurs when charging begins.

For best results when using Wireless PowerShare, please note:

- Remove any accessories or covers before using the feature. Depending on the type of accessory or cover, Wireless PowerShare may not work properly.—

- The location of the wireless charging coil may vary by device, so you may need to adjust the placement to make a connection. When charging starts, a notification or vibration will occur, so the notification will help you know you have made a connection.

- Call reception or data services may be affected, depending on your network environment.

- Charging speed or efficiency can vary depending on device condition or surrounding environment.

- Only devices that support the wireless charging feature can be charged using this feature. Some devices may not be charged.

- To charge properly, do not move or use either device while charging.

- If the remaining battery power drops below a certain level, power sharing will stop.

TURNING THE DEVICE ON AND OFF

Turning the device on

Press and hold the **Power** key for a few seconds to turn on the device.

When you turn on your device for the first time or after performing a data reset, follow the on-screen instructions to set up your device.

Turning the device off

1. To turn off the device, press and hold the **Power** key and tap **Power Off**.

   Confirm when prompted.

2. To restart the device, press and hold the **Power** key and tap **Restart**.

INITIAL SETTING UP OF GALAXY FOLD

When you turn on your device for the first time or after performing a data reset, the Setup Wizard guides you through the basics of setting up your device. Follow the prompts to choose a default language, connect to a Wi-Fi network, set up accounts, choose location services and more. After completing the setup, the Home screen will appear.

SET UP AND MANAGE YOUR ACCOUNTS

The accounts to be set up include Samsung account, Google account and your email accounts.

Set up your Samsung Account

Your Samsung account is an integrated account service that allows you to use a variety of Samsung services provided by mobile devices, TVs, and the Samsung website. If you do not have a Samsung account, you should create one. You can create a Samsung account using your email address by following the steps below.

1. Launch the **Settings** app and tap **Accounts and backup**
2. Select **Accounts**
3. Select **Add account** and tap on **Samsung account**.
4. Tap **Create account**.
5. Follow the on-screen instructions to complete creating your account.

Set up your Google Account

Adding or setting up a Google account on your device will grant you access to your Google cloud storage, apps installed from your account and features like **Factory Reset Protection** (FRP). FRP prevents other people from using your device if it is reset to factory settings without your permission. For example, if your device is lost or stolen and a factory data reset is performed, only someone with your Google Account username and password can use the device.

You can create a Google account by following the steps below.

1. Launch the **Settings** app and tap 🔑 **Accounts and backup**
2. Select **Accounts**
3. Select ✚ **Add account** and tap on **Google**.
4. Tap **Create account**.
5. Follow the on-screen instructions to complete creating your account.

Set up your email Account

Setting up and signing in to one or more of your email accounts will enable you view and manage your email messages. Follow the steps below to set up your email account.

1. Launch the **Settings** app and tap 🔑 **Accounts and backup**
2. Select **Accounts**
3. Select ✚ **Add account** and tap on **Email**.
4. Tap **Create account**.
5. Follow the on-screen instructions to complete creating your account.

TRANSFERRING DATA FROM YOUR OLD DEVICE

Use Smart Switch to seamlessly transfer contacts, photos, music, videos, messages, notes, calendars, and more from your old device to your new Galaxy Fold. Smart Switch can transfer your data via USB cable, Wi-Fi, or computer.

Transferring data via USB cable

Follow these steps to transfer data from your old device using Smart Switch via USB cable

1. Connect the two phones as shown below using the old phone's USB cable and the USB-OTG adapter that came with your new Galaxy Fold.

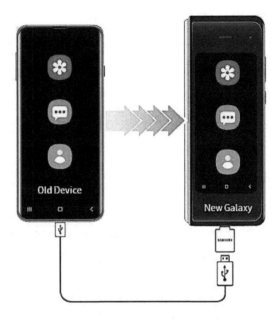

2. Launch **Smart Switch** on both devices by going to **Settings** and tap 🔑 **Accounts and backup**.

3. Tap **Send data** on the old device and tap **Cable**.

4. On your new Galaxy Fold, tap **Receive data**. Once it finishes scanning the old phone, select the data you want transferred, and then tap **Transfer**.

5. When the data transfer finishes, tap **Done** on your Galaxy Fold, and tap **Close** on the old device.

Transferring data wirelessly via Wi-Fi

Transfer data from your previous device to your device wirelessly via Wi-Fi Direct.

1. On the previous device, launch **Smart Switch**. If you do not have the app, download it from Galaxy Store.

2. On your device, go to **Settings** and tap ✎ **Accounts and backup**, then select **Smart Switch**.

3. Place the devices near each other at about 4 inches apart.

4. On the previous device, tap **Send data** and select **Wireless**. The two devices will automatically connect.

5. On the previous device, select the item(s) you want to transfer and tap **Send**.

6. On your Galaxy Fold, tap **Receive**; the data transfer will begin.

7. When the transfer is complete, tap **Done** on your Galaxy Fold, and tap **Close** on your old device.

Backing up and restoring data using external storage

Transfer data using external storage, such as a microSD card in two stages.

Backing up data

1. Insert the microSD card into your old device.

2. Launch **Smart Switch** on your previous device and tap the **SD card** icon at the upper right corner.

3. Tap **Back up** and select the items you want to back up and tap **Back up** again.

4. When it's complete, tap **Done**.

Restoring data

1. Insert the microSD card into your Galaxy Fold.

2. On your Galaxy Fold, launch the **Settings** app and tap **Accounts and backup** and select **Smart Switch**.

3. Tap the **SD card** icon and select **Restore**.

4. Select the items you want to restore and tap **Restore** again.

5. When it's complete, tap **Done**.

NAVIGATING GALAXY FOLD

The Galaxy Fold comes with a touch screen that responds best to a light touch from your finger or the S Pen. Using excessive pressure or any sharp object on the touch screen may damage the touchscreen and void the warranty.

When you turn on the screen, the navigation soft buttons will appear at the bottom of the screen. The navigation soft buttons are set to the Recents button, Home button, and Back button by default. The functions of the buttons can change according to the usage environment and may include:

- **Recents** button — Tap to open the list of recent apps.

- **Home** button — Tap to return to the Home screen.

- **Back** button — Tap to return to the previous screen.

Old

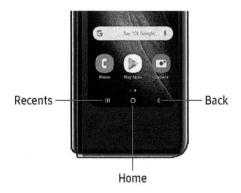

Recents ——————— III O < ——————— Back

Home

Hiding the navigation bar

You can hide the navigation bar in order to view files or use apps on a wider screen. This can be achieved by following the steps below:

1. Go to **Settings and** tap ☀ **Display**

2. Select **Navigation bar**, and then tap **Full screen gestures** under **Navigation type**.

The navigation bar will be hidden and the gesture hints will appear where the soft buttons are located. To use the soft buttons, drag the gesture hint of the desired button upwards. If you want to hide the gesture hints at the bottom of the screen, tap the **Gesture hints** switch to deactivate it.

Re-Ordering the Navigation bar soft buttons

You can personalize your Galaxy Fold navigation bar soft buttons by changing where the Recent apps and Back buttons display on the Navigation bar.

1. Go to **Settings** and tap ☀ **Display**.

2. Select **Navigation bar** and tap an option under **Button order**.

HOME SCREEN AND APPS SCREEN

The Home screen is the starting point for accessing all of the device's features. It displays widgets, app icons, and more. You can set up additional Home screens, remove screens, change the order of screens, and choose a main Home screen. While the Apps screen displays icons for all apps, including newly installed apps.

App icons

You can launch an app from any Home screen by tapping on app icons. To add an app icon to the Home screen, follow the steps below.

1. From Apps screen, touch and hold the app icon you want to add to the Home screen and tap **Add to Home**.

To remove an icon from the Home screen:

2. Touch and hold an app icon on the Home screen, and tap 🗑 **Remove from Home**.

Note that removing an icon from the Home screen does not delete the app; it only removes it from the Home screen.

Wallpapers

You can change the look of the Home and Lock screens by choosing a favorite picture or preloaded wallpaper.

1. From a Home screen, touch and hold the screen.
2. Tap 🖼 **Wallpapers**.
3. Tap an image to choose it.
4. Tap **Set as wallpaper**, and confirm when prompted.

Widgets

You can add widgets to your Home screen for quick access to information or apps.

1. From a Home screen, touch and hold the screen.
2. Tap **Widgets** icon and then touch and hold the widget that you want, drag it to the Home screen and release your hand.

LOCK OR UNLOCK YOUR DEVICE'S SCREEN

Pressing the **Power** key turns off the screen and locks it. Also, the screen turns off and automatically locks if the device is not used for a specified period. When the screen turns on, swipe in any direction to unlock the screen. If the screen is off, press the **Power** key to turn on the screen or alternatively, double-tap the screen.

Changing the screen lock method

To change the screen lock method, follow the steps below:

1. Go to **Settings** and tap **Lock screen**.
2. Tap **Screen lock type** and select the desired method.

   The Screen lock types include the following:

   • **Swipe**: Swipe in any direction on the screen to unlock it.

   • **Pattern**: Draw a pattern with four or more dots to unlock the screen.

   • **PIN**: Enter a PIN with at least four numbers to unlock the screen.

- **Password**: Enter a password with at least four characters, numbers, or symbols to unlock the screen.

- **None**: Do not set a screen lock method.

- **Face**: Register your face to unlock the screen.

- **Fingerprints**: Register your fingerprints to unlock the screen.

3. Toggle the **Notification** button **On** to enable showing notifications on the lock screen.

   The following options are available:

   - **View style**: Display notification details or hide them and show only an icon.

   - **Hide content**: Do not show notifications in the notification panel.

   - **Show on Always On Display**: Display notifications on the Always on Display screen.

4. Tap **Done** when finished.

Using Face Recognition to unlock your screen

You can set the device to unlock the screen by recognizing your face. Before using the face recognition to unlock your device, you must bear in mind that face recognition is less secure than Pattern, PIN, or Password; and your device could be unlocked by someone or something that looks like your image. Secondly, some conditions may affect face recognition, including wearing glasses, hats, beards, or heavy make-up.

Follow the steps below to register your face:

1. Ensure that you are in a well-lit area and the camera lens is clean before starting the registration.
2. Go to **Settings** and tap **Biometrics and security**.
3. Select **Face Recognition** and follow the prompts to register your face.
4. Set a screen lock method.
5. Select whether you are wearing glasses or not and tap **Continue**.
6. Hold the device with the screen facing towards you and look at the screen.
7. Position your face inside the frame on the screen. The camera will scan your face.

Deleting the registered face data

You can delete face data that you have registered.

1. On the Settings screen, tap **Biometrics and security** and select **Face recognition**.
2. Unlock the screen using the preset screen lock method.
3. Tap **Remove face data** and select **Remove**. Once the registered face is deleted, all the related features will also be deactivated.

Unlocking the screen with your face

You can unlock the screen with your face instead of using a pattern, PIN, or password.

1. On the Settings screen, tap **Biometrics and security** and select **Face recognition**.
2. Unlock the screen using the preset screen lock method.
3. Tap the **Face unlock** switch to activate it.
4. On the locked screen, look at the screen. When your face is recognized, you can unlock the screen without using any additional screen lock method. If your face is not recognized, use the preset screen lock method.

Using Fingerprint Recognition to unlock your screen

In order for fingerprint recognition to function, your fingerprint information needs to be registered and stored in your device. After registering, you can set the device to use your fingerprint for the screen lock.

Follow the steps below to register your fingerprint:
1. Go to Settings and tap **Biometrics and security**.
2. Select **Fingerprints** and follow the prompts to register your face.
3. Set a screen lock method.
4. Place your finger on the fingerprint recognition sensor at the bottom of the screen. After the device detects your finger, lift it up and place it on the fingerprint recognition sensor again. Repeat this action until the fingerprint is registered.
5. When you are finished registering your fingerprints, tap **Done**.

Checking registered fingerprints

You can check whether your fingerprint is registered by placing your finger on the fingerprint recognition sensor.

1. On the Settings screen, tap **Biometrics and security** and select **Fingerprints**.
2. Unlock the screen using the preset screen lock method.
3. Tap **Check added fingerprints**.
4. Place your finger on the fingerprint recognition sensor. The recognition result will be displayed.

Deleting registered fingerprints

You can delete registered fingerprints.

1. On the Settings screen, tap **Biometrics and security** and select **Fingerprints**.
2. Unlock the screen using the preset screen lock method.
3. Select a fingerprint to delete and tap **Remove**.

Unlocking the screen with your fingerprints

You can unlock the screen with your fingerprint instead of using a pattern, PIN, or password.

1. On the Settings screen, tap **Biometrics and security** and select **Fingerprints**.
2. Unlock the screen using the preset screen lock method.
3. Tap the **Fingerprint unlock** switch to activate it.
4. On the locked screen, place your finger on the fingerprint recognition sensor and scan your fingerprint.

NOTIFICATION PANEL

When you receive new notifications, indicator icons appear on the status bar. To see more information about the icons, open the notification panel and view the details.

1. To open the notification panel, drag the status bar downwards.

2. Swipe down the list to see notification details.

   - To open an item, tap it.

   - To clear a single notification, drag the notification left or right.

   - To clear all notifications, tap **Clear**.

   - To customize notifications, tap **Notification settings**.

3. To close the notification panel, swipe upwards from the bottom of the screen or tap Back to close the Notification panel.

Quick settings

Notification cards

Device settings

View all

APPS AND FEATURES

Installing apps

Apps may be purchased and downloaded from either Galaxy Store or Google Play Store. To install, launch the Galaxy Store or Google Play Store app. Browse apps by category or search for apps by keyword. Select an app to view information about it. To download free apps, tap **INSTALL**. To purchase and download apps where charges apply, tap the price and follow the on-screen instructions.

Uninstalling or disabling apps

Tap and hold an app and select an option.

- **Uninstall**: Uninstall downloaded apps.

- **Disable**: Disable selected default apps that cannot be uninstalled from the device.

Enabling apps

1. Go to **Settings** and tap **Apps**.

2. Click on the **Down Arrow** and select **Disabled**.

3. Select an app and then tap **Enable**.

Create and use folders

You can make folders to organize App shortcuts on the Apps list.

1. From **Apps**, touch and hold an app shortcut, and then drag it on top of another app shortcut until it is highlighted.

2. Release the app shortcut to create the folder.

   - **Enter folder name**: Name the folder.

   - **Palette**: Change the folder color.

   - **Add apps**: Place more apps in the folder. Tap apps to select them, and then tap **Add**.

3. Tap **Back** to close the folder.

Copy a folder to a Home screen

You can copy a folder to a Home screen.

- From **Apps**, touch and hold a folder, and tap **Add to Home** icon.

Delete a folder

When you delete a folder, the app shortcuts return to the **Apps** list.

1. From **Apps**, touch and hold a folder to delete.

2. Tap **Delete folder** icon, and confirm when prompted.

PHONE

The **Phone** app is a very versatile tool in the device that can do more than just make telephone calls. The Phone app allows you to make and answer calls from the **Home** screen, **Recents** tab, **Contacts** and more.

Make a call

Use your phone to make voice and video calls from a **Home** screen.

- From **Phone**, enter a number on the keypad and tap **Call** to make a voice call or **Video call** to make a video call.

   Tap **Keypad** if the keypad is not displayed.

- You can also enable swipe to make a call by swiping a contact or number to the right.

   To enable this feature, follow these steps:

   - From **Settings**, and tap **Advanced features**.

   - Select **Motions and gestures**.

   - Toggle the **Swipe to call or send messages** button to **On** to enable this feature.

Add the number to the contacts list

Access additional options

Search for a contact

Access voicemail

Make a call

Make a video call

Use your phone to make calls from **Recents**

All incoming, outgoing, and missed calls are recorded in the Call log.

1. From 🔵 **Phone**, tap **Recents** to display a list of recent calls.

2. Tap a contact, and then tap **Call**.

Use your phone to make calls from **Contacts**

You can call a contact from the **Contacts** app.

• From 🔵 **Contacts**, swipe your finger across a contact to the right to call the contact.

Answer a call

When a call is received, the phone rings and the caller's phone number or name is displayed. If you are using an app, a pop-up screen is displayed for the incoming call.

- On the incoming call screen, drag **Answer** to the right to answer the call.
- On the incoming call pop-up screen, tap **Answer** icon to answer the call.

Decline a call

You can choose to decline an incoming call. If you are using an app, a pop-up screen is displayed for the incoming call.

- On the incoming call screen, drag **Decline** to the left to reject the call and send it to your voicemail.
- On the incoming pop-up screen, tap **Decline** to reject the call and send it to your voicemail.

Decline with a message

You can choose to decline an incoming call with a text message response.

- On the incoming call screen, drag **Send message** upward and select a message.
- On the incoming call pop-up screen, tap **Send message** and select a message.

End a call

- Tap 🔘 **End** when you are ready to end your call.

Manage calls

Your calls are recorded in a call log. You can set up speed dials, block numbers, and use voicemail.

Call log

The numbers of the calls you have dialed, received, or missed are stored in the **Call log**.

- From 📞 **Phone**, tap **Recents**. A list of recent calls is displayed. If the caller is in your **Contacts** list, the caller's name is displayed.

Save a contact from a recent call

Use recent call information to create a contact or update your **Contacts** list.

1. From 📞 **Phone**, tap **Recents**.
2. Tap the call that contains the information that you want to save to your **Contacts** list, and tap ➕ **Add to contacts**.
3. Tap **Create contact** or **Update existing**.

Delete call records

To delete **Call log** entries:

1. From 📞 **Phone**, tap **Recents**.
2. Touch and hold the call you want to delete from the Call log.

3. Tap 🗑 **Delete**.

Block a number

By adding a caller to your Block list, future calls from this number are sent directly to your voicemail, and messages are not received.

1. From 🅲 **Phone**, tap **Recents**.

2. Tap the caller you want to add to the Block list.

3. Tap ⓘ **Details**, select 🚫 **Block**, and confirm when prompted.

Speed dial

You can assign a shortcut number to a contact for speed dialing their default number.

1. From 🅲 **Phone** and tap Keypad.

2. Select ⋮ **More options** and tap **Speed dial numbers**. The Speed dial numbers screen displays the reserved speed dial numbers.

3. Tap an unassigned number.

    • Tap ▼ **Menu** to select a different Speed dial number than the next one in sequence.

    • Number 1 is reserved for Voicemail.

4. Type in a name or number, or tap 👤 **Add from Contacts** to assign a contact to the number.

    1. The selected contact is displayed in the Speed dial number box.

Make a call with Speed dial

To make a call, tap and hold a speed dial number on the keypad from **Phone**. For speed dial numbers 10 and up, tap the first digit(s) of the number, and then tap and hold the last digit. For example, if you set the number 123 as a speed dial number, tap 1, tap 2, and then tap and hold 3.

Remove a Speed dial number

You can remove an assigned Speed dial number.

1. From 🇨 **Phone**, tap ⋮ **More options** and select **Speed dial numbers**.

2. Tap ➖ **Remove** by the contact you want to remove from Speed dial.

Voicemail

You can set up your voicemail service when you access it for the first time by following the tutorial to create a password, record a greeting, and record your name. You can always follow the steps below to access voicemail through the Phone app.

1. From 🇨 **Phone**, tap 📧 **Voicemail** or from Apps, tap 📧 **Visual Voicemail**.

2. Follow the voice prompts from the voicemail center.

CONTACTS

You can store and manage contacts on your device.

To create contacts on your device, follow these steps:

1. From Apps, select Contacts and tap Create contact.

2. Select a storage location.

3. Enter contact information and tap **Save**.

Edit a contact

When editing a contact, you can tap a field and change or delete information, or you can add more fields to the contact's list of information.

1. From Contacts, tap a contact.
2. Tap Edit.
3. Tap any of the fields to add, change, or delete information.
4. Tap **Save**.

Call or message a contact

You can quickly call or message a contact using their default phone number.

1. From Contacts, tap a contact.
2. Tap Call or Message.

Import contacts

You can add contacts by importing them from other storages to your device.

1. From 😊 **Contacts**, tap ☰ **Menu** and select **Manage contacts**.

2. Tap **Import/export contacts**.

3. Tap **Import** and select a storage location to import contacts from.

4. Tick **VCF files** or contacts to import and tap **Done**.

5. Select a storage location to save contacts to and tap **Import**.

Export contacts

You can manually back up your contacts to an installed memory card.

1. From 😊 **Contacts**, tap ☰ **Menu** and select **Manage contacts**.

2. Tap **Import/export contacts**.

3. Tap **Export** and follow the prompts.

Delete contacts

You can delete a single contact or multiple contacts.

1. From 😊 **Contacts**, touch and hold a contact to select it.

   • You can also tap multiple contacts to select them for deletion.

2. Tap 🗑 **Delete**, and confirm when prompted.

MESSAGES

Send a message

1. Launch the 💬 **Messages** app and tap ⚪ **Compose**.

2. Add recipients and enter a message.

3. Tap ⬈ to send the message.

Message search

To quickly locate a message, use the search feature.

1. From 💬 **Messages**, tap 🔍 **Search**.

2. Enter keywords in the **Search** field, and then tap 🔍 **Search** on the keyboard.

Delete conversations

You can remove your conversion history by deleting conversations.

1. From 💬 **Messages**, tap ⋮ **More options** and select **Edit**.

2. Tap each conversation you want to delete.

3. Tap 🗑 **Delete**, and confirm when prompted.

Send SOS messages

You can send a message with your location to designated contacts when in an emergency situation.

1. Go to **Settings and** tap ✳ **Advanced features**.

2. Toggle the **Send SOS messages** button to enable this feature.

3. Tap **Send messages to** and select **Add to** add recipients by creating new contacts or selecting from Contacts.

- To include a picture from your front and rear camera, tap **Attach pictures**.

- To include a five-second audio recording in your SOS message, tap **Attach audio recording**.

4. Press the **Power** key quickly three times to send an SOS message.

INTERNET

Browsing webpages

Browse the Internet to search for information and bookmark your favorite webpages to access them conveniently.

1. Launch the ◯ **Internet** app.
2. Tap the address field.
3. Enter the web address or a keyword, and then tap **Go**.

Browser tabs

You can use tabs to view multiple web pages at the same time.

- From ◯ **Internet**, tap ⬜ **Tabs** and select **New tab**.
  o To close a tab, tap ⬜ Tabs and select ✕ **Close tab**.

Bookmarks

The Bookmarks page stores Bookmarks, Saved pages, and your browsing History.

Open a Bookmark

Follow these steps to quickly launch a web page from the Bookmarks page.

1. From ⬤ **Internet**, tap ⭐ **Bookmarks**.
2. Tap a bookmark entry.

Save a web page

Saving a web page stores its content on your device so that you can access it offline.

1. Go to ⬤ **Internet** and tap ☰ .
2. Select **Add page to** and tap **Saved pages**.

- To view saved web pages, tap ☰ and select **Saved pages**.

View browsing history

To view a list of recently visited web pages:

- Go to ⬤ **Internet**, tap ☰ and select **History**.

CAMERA

You can capture high-quality pictures and videos using the **Camera** app. There are two ways to launch the Camera app: from Apps and from Quick launch (if enabled).

- From **Apps**, tap 📷 **Camera**.
- If **Quick launch** is enabled, quickly press the **Power** key twice.

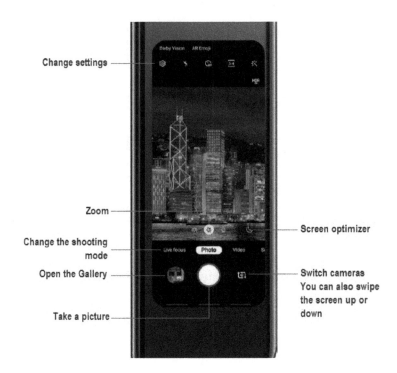

Change settings

Zoom

Screen optimizer

Change the shooting
mode

Open the Gallery

Switch cameras
You can also swipe
the screen up or
down

Take a picture

Take a picture

Follow these steps to take stunning pictures with your device's front
and rear cameras.

1. From 📷 **Camera**, set up your shot with the following
features:

- Tap the screen where you want the camera to focus.
When you tap the screen, a brightness scale appears. Drag the 💡
light bulb to adjust the brightness.

- To quickly switch between the front and rear cameras,
swipe the screen up or down.

- To change to a different shooting mode, swipe the screen
right or left.

- To change camera settings, tap ⚙ **Settings**.

2. Tap ◯ **Capture**.

Camera Features

Galaxy Fold has several camera features that are designed to produce better and more professional pictures.

Super Slow-mo

This feature enables you record video at a high frame for viewing in high quality slow motion

1. From 📷 **Camera**, swipe left to **Super slow-mo**.
2. Tap ◉ **Super Slow-mo** to record.

AR Emoji

This camera feature enables you turn yourself into an emoji that you can add to text messages.

1. From 📷 **Camera**, tap **AR Emoji** and select **Create my emoji**.
2. Tap ◯ **Capture**, and follow the prompts to create your emoji.

Other features include:

- **Food**: Take pictures that emphasize the vivid colors of food.
- **Panorama**: Create a linear image by taking pictures in either a horizontal or vertical direction.
- **Pro**: Manually adjust the ISO sensitivity, exposure value, white balance, and color tone while taking pictures.

- **Live focus**: Take artistic pictures by adjusting the depth of field.

- **Slow motion**: Record videos at a high frame rate for viewing in slow motion.

- **Hyperlapse**: Create a time lapse video by recording at various frame rates. The frame rate is adjusted depending on the scene being recorded and the movement of the device.

Camera settings

You can use the icons on the main camera screen and the settings menu to configure your camera's settings. This section will help you configure the camera's intelligent features, pictures, videos and other useful features.

- From **Camera**, tap **Settings** for the following options:
  Intelligent features

  - **Scene optimizer**: Automatically adjust the color settings of your pictures to match the subject matter.

  - **Shot suggestions**: Get tips to help you choose the best shooting mode.

  - **Flaw detection**: Receive warning when someone blinks, the subject is not in focus, or the lens needs cleaning.

  Pictures

  - **Motion photos**: Create a short video by taking pictures.

- **Hold shutter button to**: Choose whether to take a picture, take a burst shot, or create a GIF when holding the shutter button down.

- **Save options**: Choose picture format and whether to flip your selfies.

Videos

- **Rear video size**: Select a resolution. Selecting a higher resolution for higher quality requires more memory.

- **Front video size**: Select a resolution. Selecting a higher resolution for higher quality requires more memory.

- **Advanced recording options**: Choose to record in either HDR10+ or HEVC formats.

- **Video stabilization**: Activate anti-shake to keep the focus steady when the camera is moving.

Useful features

- **HDR (rich tone)**: Enables the light sensitivity and color depth features of the device to produce a brighter and richer picture.

- **Tracking auto-focus**: Keep a moving subject in focus.

- **Grid lines**: Display viewfinder grid lines to help compose a picture or video.

- **Location tags**: Attach a GPS location tag to the picture.

- **Camera modes**: Set the default camera mode. You can also reorder or hide your shooting modes.
- **Shooting methods**:
  - **Press Volume key to**: Use the Volume key to take pictures, record video, zoom, or control system volume.
  - **Voice control**: Take pictures speaking key words.
  - **Floating shutter button**: Add an extra shutter button that you can move anywhere on the screen.
  - **Show palm**: Hold your hand out with your palm facing the camera to have your picture taken in a few seconds.
- **Quick launch**: Press the Power key twice in quick succession to open the camera.
- **Quick review**: Review pictures after taking them.
- **Shutter sound**: Play a tone when taking a picture.
- **Reset settings**: Reset the camera settings.
- **About Camera**: View app and software information.

GALLERY

Galaxy Fold Gallery enables you to view, edit, and manage pictures and videos.

View pictures

You can view pictures stored on your device in the Gallery app. To view pictures, follow the steps below:

1. From ✱ **Gallery**, tap **Pictures**.

2. Tap a picture to view it. Swipe left or right to view other pictures or videos.

   • To mark the picture as a favorite, tap ♡ **Favorite**.

   • To use Bixby Vision on the current picture, tap **Bixby Vision**.

   • To access the following features, tap ⋮ **More options**:

     – **Details**: View and edit information about the picture.

     – **Set as wallpaper**: Set the picture as wallpaper.

     – **Set as Always On Display image**: Set the picture as the background image for the Always On Display.

     – **Move to Secure Folder**: Move the picture to a Secure Folder.

     – **Print**: Send the picture to a connected printer.

Edit pictures

You can enhance your pictures using the Gallery's editing tools.

1. From ✱ **Gallery**, tap **Pictures**.

2. Tap a picture to view it, and then tap ✎ **Edit** for the following options:

- ⬜ **Transform**: Rotate, flip, crop, or make other changes to the overall appearance of the picture.

- ⊛ **Effects**: Add color effects.

- 🙂 **Stickers**: Overlay illustrated or animated stickers.

- T **Text**: Add text to the picture.

- 🎨 **Draw**: Add handwritten text or hand drawn content.

- ☀ **Brightness**: Adjust brightness image controls.

Play video

You can view the videos stored on your device. You can also save videos as favorites, and view video details.

1. From ✳ **Gallery**, tap **Pictures**.

2. Tap a video to view it. Swipe left or right to view other pictures or videos.

   - To mark the video as a favorite, tap ♡ **Favorite**. The video is added to Favorites under the Albums tab.

   - To access the following features, tap ⋮ **More options**:

     – **Details**: View and edit information about the video.

     – **Set as wallpaper**: Set the video as wallpaper on the Lock screen.

     – **Move to Secure Folder**: Add this video to your Secure Folder.

3. Tap ▶ **Play video** to play the video.

Edit video

This feature enables you to edit videos stored on your device.

1. From ✷ **Gallery**, tap **Pictures**.

2. Tap a video to view it.

3. Tap ✐ **Edit** to use the following tools:

   - ↻ **Rotate**: Rotate the video clockwise.

   - ✂ **Trim**: Cut segments of the video.

   - ⊗ **Effects**: Add visual effects to the video.

   - ◐ **Beauty face**: Enhance faces.

   - ☺ **Sticker**: Overlay illustrated or animated stickers.

   - ♪ **Audio**: Adjust the volume levels and add background music to the video.

4. Tap **Save**, and confirm when prompted.

Delete pictures and videos

To delete pictures and videos stored on your device, follow these steps:

1. From ✷ **Gallery**, tap ⋮ **More options** and select **Edit**.

2. Tap pictures and videos to select them, or tap the **All** checkbox at the top of the screen to select all pictures and videos.

3. Tap 🗑 **Delete**, and confirm when prompted.

MY FILES

You can view and manage files stored on your device, including images, videos, music, and sound clips.

- To launch My Files, go to **Apps**, tap **Samsung** folder and select ⬜ **My Files**.

My Files options

The options available on My Files can enable to search, edit, clear file history, and more.

- From ⬜ **My Files**, the following options are available:

  - 🔍 **Search**: Search for a file or folder.

  - ⋮ **More options**:

    - Clear recent files: Remove the list of recently accessed files. This option is only available after a file has been opened through My Files.

    - Storage analysis: See what's taking up space in your storage.

    - Settings: View settings for the app.

MULTI WINDOW

There are times you wish you had two devices - that way, you could send an email on one but read an article on another. With split screen view, you can do that with just one device on Galaxy Fold. Multi window feature lets you open two apps on your device and use them simultaneously, so you can multitask more easily and faster than ever. You can also run multiple apps at the same time in the split screen view.

To open multiple apps in split screen view, follow these steps:

1. From any screen, tap ||| **Recent apps** to open the list of recently used apps.

2. Tap an app's icon, and then tap **Open in split screen view**. The selected app will launch in one of the window.

3. Tap another app in the other window to add it to the split screen view.

    - Drag the middle of the window border to adjust the window size.

SAMSUNG NOTES

Samsung Notes are used to create notes containing text, images with footnotes, voice recordings, and music.

- Go to **Settings** and tap 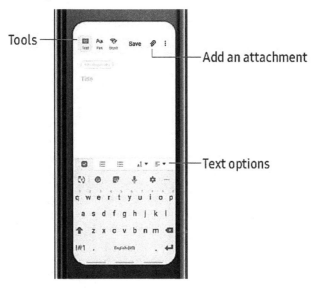 **Samsung Notes**.
- Select **Create**.

Tools ——————
Add an attachment

Text options

Notes menu

You can view your notes by category.

- From **Samsung Notes**, tap ≡ **Menu** for the following options:
  - **All notes**: View all notes.
  - **Frequently used**: Quick access to commonly used notes.
  - **Trash**: View deleted notes.
  - **Categories**: View notes by category.
  - **Settings**: View settings for the Samsung Notes app.

Notes options

You can edit, share, or manage notes.

- From **Samsung Notes**, tap ⋮ **More options** icon for the following options:

    - **Edit**: Select notes to share, delete, or move.

    - **Sort**: Change the way notes are organized.

    - **View**: Switch between Grid, List, or Simple list.

Edit notes

Follow these steps to make edits to notes you already created.

1. From **Samsung Notes**, tap a note to view it.
2. Tap **Edit**, and make changes. When you are finished, tap **Save**.

SETTINGS

CONNECTIONS

You can change settings for various connections, such as the Wi-Fi feature and Bluetooth, between your device and a variety of networks and other devices.

Wi-Fi

You can activate the Wi-Fi feature to connect to a Wi-Fi network and access the Internet or other network devices without using your mobile data.

To connect to a Wi-Fi network, follow the steps below:

1. On the **Settings** screen, tap **Connections**, select **Wi-Fi** and toggle the button to activate it.

2. Scan for available networks and select a network from the Wi-Fi networks list. Networks that require a password appear with a lock icon. Enter the password and tap **Connect**.

3. Once the device connects to a Wi-Fi network, the device will reconnect to that network each time it is available without requiring a password. To prevent the device connecting to the network automatically, select it from the list of networks and tap **Forget**.

Wi-Fi Direct

Wi-Fi Direct connects devices directly via a Wi-Fi network without requiring an access point.

1. On the **Settings** screen, tap **Connections**, select **Wi-Fi** and toggle the button to activate it.

2. Tap **Wi-Fi Direct**. The detected devices are listed but if the device you want to connect to is not in the list, request that the device turns on its Wi-Fi Direct feature.

3. Select a device to connect to. The devices will be connected when the other device accepts the Wi-Fi Direct connection request.

Ending the device connection

1. On the Settings screen, tap 🛜 **Connections** and select **Wi-Fi**.

2. Tap **Wi-Fi Direct**. The device displays the connected devices in the list.

3. Tap the device name to disconnect the devices.

Bluetooth

Use Bluetooth to exchange data or media files with other Bluetooth-enabled devices.

Pairing with other Bluetooth devices

1. On the Settings screen, tap 🛜 **Connections**, and toggle the 🔵 **Bluetooth** button to activate it. The detected devices will be listed.

2. Select a device to pair with. If the device you want to pair with is not on the list, set the device to enter Bluetooth pairing mode.

3. Accept the Bluetooth connection request on your device to confirm. The devices will be connected when the other device accepts the Bluetooth connection request.

Rename a paired device

You can rename a paired device to make it easier to recognize.

1. From Settings, tap 📶 **Connections**, and toggle the 🔵 **Bluetooth** button to activate it. The detected devices will be listed.
1. Tap ⚙️ **Settings** next to the device name, and then tap **Rename**.
2. Enter a new name, and tap **Rename**.

Dual audio

You can connect up to two Bluetooth audio devices to your tablet. Connect two Bluetooth headsets or speakers to use them at the same time.

1. From Settings, tap 📶 **Connections**, and toggle the 🔵 **Bluetooth** button to activate it. The detected devices will be listed.
2. Tap ⋮ **More options**, select **Advanced**, tap the **Dual audio** switch to activate it, and then tap the **Back** button.

3. Select a device to pair with. If the device you want to pair with is not in the list, turn on its visibility option or enter Bluetooth pairing mode on the device.

4. Tap ⚙ **Settings** next to the connected device and tap the **Audio** button to activate it.

5. Select another device from the list and activate its **Audio** feature.

Unpairing Bluetooth devices

1. From Settings, tap 📶 **Connections**, and toggle the ✷ **Bluetooth** button to activate it. The detected devices will be listed.

2. Tap ⚙ **Settings** next to the connected device and tap **Unpair**.

Mobile networks

Mobile networks feature enables you to configure your device's ability to connect to mobile networks and use mobile data. To configure your device to use mobile data to access internet, do the following:

- Go to **Settings**, tap 📶 **Connections** and select **Mobile networks**.

- Toggle the **Mobile data** button to enable mobile data usage.

Mobile hotspot

You can use mobile hotspot to share your device's mobile data connection with other devices through Wi-Fi network.

1. On the **Settings** screen, tap 📶 **Connections**, select **Mobile Hotspot and Tethering**; and **tap Mobile Hotspot**.

2. Toggle **Mobile hotspot** button to activate it. Other devices can find your device in the Wi-Fi networks list.

   • To set a password for the mobile hotspot, from the **Mobile Hotspot** page, tap ⋮ **More options** and click **Configure Mobile Hotspot**.

   • Tap Password and select **Change** password. On the **Change password** field, enter the desired password and tap **Save**.

3. On the devices you want to connect, search for and select your device from the Wi-Fi networks list.

4. On the connected device, use the device's mobile data connection to access the Internet.

Tethering

You can use tethering to share your device's Internet connection with a computer.

1. From **Settings**, tap 📶 **Connections** and select **Mobile hotspot and tethering**.

2. Connect the computer to the device using a USB cable, and then tap **USB tethering**.

Connect to a printer

You can connect the device to a printer via Wi-Fi or Wi-Fi Direct, and print images or documents. To use this feature, you have to add the printer plug-ins for printer(s) you want to connect the device to. Follow these steps to add printer plug-ins:

1. From **Settings**, tap 📶 **Connections** and select **More connection settings**.

2. Tap **Printing** and select ➕ **Download plugin**. Follow the prompts to add a print service.

3. Tap the print service, and then tap ⋮ **More options**.

4. Select **Add printer**.

DISPLAY

This feature enables you to configure the screen brightness, font size and other display settings.

Screen brightness

You can adjust the screen brightness according to lighting conditions or personal preference.

1. From **Settings**, tap ☼ **Display**.

2. Customize options under **Brightness**:

   - Drag the **Brightness** slider to set a custom brightness level.

   - Tap **Adaptive brightness** to automatically adjust the screen brightness based on the lighting conditions.

– **Reset usage patterns**: Clear your brightness adjustment history. Your device begins learning your preferences again after the reset.

Night mode

Night mode allows you to switch to a darker theme to keep your eyes more comfortable at night.

- From **Settings**, tap ⚙ **Display** and select **Night mode** for the following options:
  - ○ **Turn on now**: Put your device in Night mode.
  - ○ **Turn on as scheduled**: Configure Night mode for either **Sunset to sunrise** or **Custom schedule**.

Font size and style

You can change the font size and style to customize your device.

- From **Settings**, tap ⚙ **Display** and select **Font size and style** for the following options:
  - ○ Drag the **Font size** slider to adjust the size of text.
  - ○ Tap **Font style** to choose a different font.
    - – Tap a font to select it, or tap ➕ **Download fonts** to add fonts from Galaxy Store.
- Tap **Bold font** to make all fonts appear with bold weight.

Full screen apps

You can choose which apps you want to use in the full screen aspect ratio.

- From **Settings**, tap ☼ **Display** and select **Full screen apps** and tap apps to enable this feature.

Continue apps on the front screen

You can choose which apps you want to continue using on the front screen when you close your device.

- From **Settings**, tap ☼ **Display** and select **Continue apps on front screen**, and tap apps to enable this feature.

Accidental touch protection

Enabling this feature will prevent the screen from detecting touch input while the device is in a dark place, such as a pocket or a bag.

- From **Settings**, tap ☼ **Display** and select **Accidental touch protection** to enable or disable the feature.

Screensaver

You can set to display images as a screensaver when the screen turns off automatically. The screensaver will be displayed when the device is charging.

1. From **Settings**, tap ☼ **Display** and select **Screen saver**.
2. Toggle the Screen saver button to enable the feature and configure the following options:
   - **Colors**: Tap the selector to display a changing screen of colors.
   - **Photo table**: Display pictures in a photo table.
   - **Photo frame**: Display pictures in a photo frame.

- **Photos**: Display pictures from your Google Photos account.

3. Tap **Preview** for a demonstration of the selected Screen saver.

Lift to wake

You can turn on the screen by lifting the device.

- From **Settings**, tap ✲ **Advanced features** and select **Motions and gestures**.

- Toggle **Lift to wake** button to enable the feature.

Double tap to wake up

You can turn on the screen by double-tapping instead of using the Power button.

- From **Settings**, tap ✲ **Advanced features** and select **Motions and gestures**.

- Toggle **Double tap to wake** button to enable the feature.

Smart stay

Smart stay feature uses the front camera to detect your face so that the screen stays on while you are looking at it.

- From **Settings**, tap ✲ **Advanced features** and select **Motions and gestures**.

- Toggle **Smart stay** button to enable the feature.

ACCESSIBILITY

Galaxy Fold is meant to be used by everyone. If you have some kind of impairment, you can feel assured that your foldable device has built-in Accessibility settings to make it easier to use. There are accessibility settings for people who need help seeing, hearing, or otherwise operating their device.

Screen Reader

Use special controls and settings that let you navigate without needing to see the screen.

1. From **Settings**, tap 👤 **Accessibility** and select **Screen reader**.

2. Tap any of the options:

   - **Voice assistant**: Receive spoken feedback when using your device, such as what you touch, select, or activate.

   - **Tutorial**: Lean how to use Voice assistant.

   - **Settings**: Configure Voice assistant to better assist you.

Visibility enhancements

You can configure Accessibility features to assist with visual aspects of your device.

Colors and clarity

You can adjust the colors and contrast of text and other screen elements for easier viewing.

- From **Settings**, tap 👤 **Accessibility** and select **Visibility enhancements**.

- Tap any of the options:

o **High contrast theme**: Adjust colors and screen fonts to increase the contrast for easier viewing.

o **High contrast fonts**: Adjust the color and outline of fonts to increase the contrast with the background.

o **High contrast keyboard**: Adjust the size of the Samsung keyboard and change its colors to increase the contrast between the keys and the background.

o **Show button shapes**: Show buttons with shaded backgrounds to make them stand out better against the wallpaper.

o **Negative colors**: Reverse the display of colors from white text on a black background to black text on a white background.

o **Color adjustment**: Adjust the color of the screen if you find it difficult to see some colors.

o **Color lens**: Adjust the screen colors if you have difficulty reading the text.

o **Remove animations**: Remove certain screen effects if you are sensitive to motion.

Size and zoom

You can increase the size of supported screen elements and create shortcuts for accessibility features on your device.

- From **Settings**, tap 🧍 **Accessibility** and select **Visibility enhancements**.

- Tap any of the options:

  o **Magnifier window**: Magnify content shown on the screen.

  o **Magnification**: Use exaggerated gestures such as triple-tapping, double pinching, and dragging two fingers across the screen.

  o **Large mouse/touchpad pointer**: Use a large pointer for a connected mouse or touchpad

  o **Font size and style**: Configure screen fonts.

  o **Screen zoom**: Configure the screen zoom level.

Hearing Enhancements

You can configure Accessibility features to assist with audial aspects of the device.

Sounds

You can adjust audio quality when using hearing aids or earphones. 🧍

- From **Settings**, tap **Accessibility** and select **Hearing enhancements**.

- Tap any of the options:

  o **Real time text**: Activate real-time text (RTT) calling.

  o **Sound detectors**: Receive alerts when the device detects a baby crying or a doorbell.

- o **Mute all sounds**: Turn off all notifications and audio for privacy.
- o **Hearing aid support**: Improve the sound quality to work better with hearing aids.
- o **Left/right sound balance**: Use the slider to adjust the left and right balance when listening to audio in stereo.
- o **Mono audio**: Switch audio from stereo to mono when using one earphone.

Text display

You can convert speech to text and watch closed captions when viewing multimedia.

- From **Settings**, tap **Accessibility** and select **Hearing enhancements**.
- Tap any of the options:
  - o **Samsung subtitles (CC)**: Use Samsung subtitles with multimedia files when available.
  - o **Google subtitles (CC)**: Use Google subtitles with multimedia files when available.
  - o **Speech-to-text**: Use the microphone to record speech and convert it to text.

Interaction and dexterity

Some people just function better when they use their hands. If you are one of those people, you can set up your device to make controlling it easier. Follow the steps below to assist with limited dexterity when interacting with your device.

- From **Settings**, tap ⚇ **Accessibility** and select **Interaction and dexterity**.
- Tap any of the options:
  - **Answering and ending calls**:
    - **Read caller names aloud**: Hear callers' names read aloud when using Galaxy Buds earbuds.
    - **Press Volume up to answer**: Use the Volume keys to answer calls.
    - **Answer automatically**: Answer calls after a set duration when using Galaxy buds earbuds.
    - **Press Power key to end**: End calls by pressing the **Power** key.

  - **Easy screen turn on**: Turn on the screen by laying it flat and moving your hand over the screen instead of using the Power button.
  - **Interaction control**: Customize areas of screen interactions, hardkeys, and the keyboard.

SAMSUNG GALAXY FOLD TIPS & TRICKS

The Galaxy Fold just as the name implies, is not just a smartphone. It's a hybrid foldable device that combines smartphone and tablet features in one device. It folds up to a small screen but when open, you have a 7.3 inch display that's great for multitasking. Here are some of the tips and tricks to enable you get the best out of your Galaxy Fold.

How to customize your Home screens

1. From a Home screen, touch and hold the screen.
2. Tap Home screen settings to customize:

   - **Home screen layout**: Set your device to have separate Home and Apps screens, or only a Home screen where all apps are located.

   - **Home screen grid**: Choose a layout to determine how icons are arranged on the Home screen.

   - **Apps screen grid**: Choose a layout to determine how icons are arranged on the Apps screen.

   - **Apps button**: Add a button to the Home screen for easy access to the Apps screen.

   - **App icon badges**: Enable to show badges on apps with active notifications. You can also choose the badge style.

   - **Lock Home screen layout**: Prevent items on the Home screen from being removed or repositioned.

- **Add apps to Home screen**: Automatically add newly-downloaded apps to the Home screen.

- **Quick-open notification panel**: Enable this feature to open the Notification panel by swiping down anywhere on the Home screen.

- **Rotate to landscape mode**: Rotate the Home screen automatically when your device's orientation is changed from portrait to landscape.

- **Hide apps**: Choose apps to hide from the Home and App screens. Return to this screen to restore hidden apps. Hidden apps are still installed and can appear as results in Finder searches.

- **About Home screen**: View version information.

How to Enable or Disable Easy Mode

The Easy mode simplifies the device's user interface by replacing the default Samsung screen layout with a simpler layout. The Easy mode simpler layout when enabled has larger text and icons. This includes size for settings, notification panel, Home screen icons and apps like Contacts, Messages, etc.

To enable the Easy mode, follow these steps:

1. Go to **Settings** and tap **Display**.
2. Tap **Easy mode**.
3. Select **Easy mode** on the next screen to enable this feature.
4. Tap **Apply** to confirm. Press the Home button to view the changes.

To disable the Easy mode, follow these steps:

1. Go to **Settings** and tap **Display**.

2. Tap **Easy mode**.

3. Select **Standard mode** on the next screen to disable the Easy mode feature.

4. Tap **Apply** to confirm.

How to Enable Lockdown mode

Lockdown Mode works by blocking all biometric security and voice recognition through Smart Lock or Bixby Voice. Once the lockdown has been activated, the only way unlock your Galaxy device is through the primary PIN, Pattern or Password. When you have enabled Lockdown mode, all notifications that would usually be displayed on the Lock Screen are hidden and can only be viewed once you have unlocked your device.

To enable Lockdown mode, follow these steps:

1. Go to **Settings** and tap **Lock screen**.

2. Tap **Secure lock settings**.

3. Toggle the **Show Lockdown option** button to **On** to enable this feature.

To use Lockdown mode, follow these steps:

- Hold down on the **Power/Lock** button, then select **Lockdown mode**.

How to enable Always On Display (AOD) feature

Always On Display is a special feature available on Galaxy Fold which helps you to view missed calls, messages alerts, check time and date without unlocking your device.

To enable this feature, follow the steps below:

1. Go to **Settings**, and tap **Lock screen**.

2. Toggle the **Always On Display** option button to **On** to select any of the options.

   - **Display mode**: Customize when to show the AOD.

   - **Screen orientation**: Display the AOD in portrait or landscape mode.

   - **Show music information**: Show music details when the FaceWidgets music controller is in use.

   - **Auto brightness**: Automatically adjust the brightness of Always On Display.

   - **About Always On Display**: View the current software version and license information.

3. Press the **back arrow** key to apply changes.

How to switch between the cameras

The Galaxy Fold is designed with six cameras and each has a specific purpose, giving you the functionality of several cameras in one device. The cameras thus: 3 rear cameras (16 MP Ultra Wide, 12 MP Wide and 12 MP Telephoto), 1 front camera (10 MP UHD Selfie) and 2 inner front cameras (10 MP UHD Selfie and 8 MP RGB Depth).

When you open the **Camera** app the camera will be facing the same direction as when it was last used, even if you have closed the app. To switch, follow these steps:

1. Tap the **Camera** app on the front screen.
2. The first camera that opens is the 12 MP Wide lens, perfect for capturing the details of something close by.
3. Tap 🕸 to swap to the 16MP Ultra Wide camera. This lens has a huge field of view, making it ideal for landscapes and panoramas.
4. Tap ◊ swap to the 12 MP Telephoto camera. This is perfect for zooming in to get vibrant close ups.
5. **Swipe up** on the screen or tap 📷 to change to the front facing camera.

   The camera that opens is the 10 MP UHD selfie camera. The shot will be close up, great for taking solo selfies.
6. Tap 👥 to zoom the camera out, fantastic for taking group selfies.
7. **Unfold** your device to continue taking pictures using the inner screen. This gives you a huge display so that you can get the best possible shot.

   The camera app will remember what you were doing on the front screen, so for this example it will open in selfie mode. The inner screen has dual front facing cameras, making it even better for snapping selfies.
8. **Swipe up** or tap 📷 to use the rear cameras

How to instantly unlock screen with the Fingerprint Sensor

By default, you have to press the **Power** button followed by pressing your finger on the fingerprint sensor to unlock your Galaxy Fold screen. Here is a tip to bypass the power button and allow you just to set your finger on the fingerprint sensor and go instantly to the home screen.

1. Go to **Settings**, tap **Biometrics and Security** and select **Fingerprints**.
2. Turn **Fingerprint Always On** to **On**. This will enable the feature.

Now, you can rest your finger on the fingerprint sensor to unlock the phone.

How to switch keyboard input language

If you're multilingual or learning a new language, you can use more than one language for your on-screen keyboard. But first, you'll need to add the other languages you want to use.

1. Go to **Settings** and tap **Language and input**.
2. Tap **On-screen keyboard**, and then tap **Samsung Keyboard**.
3. Tap **Languages and types**, and then tap **Manage input languages**.
4. Select or download from the available languages for Samsung keyboard.

To switch the keyboard's input language, open an app that uses the keyboard. Then, swipe the spacebar left or right to switch the language input.

How to use two separate accounts for the same app (Dual Messenger)

Dual Messenger capability letts you use two different accounts with one chatting app. That means you can keep your accounts for work and home separate, but on the same phone. Follow these steps to activate Dual Messenger on your device:

1. From **Settings**, tap   **Advanced features** and select **Dual messenger**.

2. Tap   next to supported apps to enable the feature for each app.

   - To select which contacts have access to the secondary messenger app, tap **Use separate contacts list**.

How to reset Galaxy Fold to factory settings

If you are having issues with your device, you may need to perform a Factory data reset. A Factory data reset will restore the device back to factory settings. It will permanently erase all personal data, preferences, settings and content such as pictures, ringtones and apps that are saved to the device. It is recommended that you save or backup important data before proceeding.

1. Go to **Settings** and tap **General management**.

2. Tap **Reset** and select **Factory data reset**.

3. Scroll to and select **Reset**.

4. Select **Delete all**.

How to know your device model, serial number and IMEI

You can view information about your Galaxy Fold by following these steps:

1. From **Settings**, tap **About phone** and then view your **phone number, model, serial number** and **IMEI** information.

2. Tap additional items to view more information about your device.

www.ingramcontent.com/pod-product-compliance
Lightning Source LLC
Chambersburg PA
CBHW070854070326
40690CB00009B/1844